ST. GREGORY'S SCHOOL
HARRY ROSE ROAD
COVENTRY
CV2 5AT

-5 DEC 1995

WHERE I LIVE
FARMING VILLAGE

**Philip Steele
meets
Eirwen Foulkes**

WATTS BOOKS
LONDON • NEW YORK • SYDNEY

©1994 Watts Books

Watts Books
96 Leonard Street
London
EC2A 4RH

Franklin Watts Australia
14 Mars Road
Lane Cove
NSW 2066

UK ISBN: 0 7496 1593 1

Dewey Decimal Classification Number 307.72

10 9 8 7 6 5 4 3 2 1

A CIP catalogue record for this book is available from the British Library.

Series editor: Belinda Weber
Editor: Nicola Baxter
Photographer: Robert Williams
Designer: Amanda Hawkes

Additional photographs: Philip Steele, Gwynedd Archive Services, Magma/Robert Williams, Sianel Pedwar Cymru/Steve Benbow, Dr John Glyn Jones

Acknowledgements: the author and publisher wish to thank John and Eirwen Foulkes, Jack, Elin and Sara; Bethan Roberts (organiser, Anglesey Young Farmers); the many people of Penmynydd and district who helped with this book.

Printed in Malaysia

CONTENTS

Where I live	4
Housing	8
Neighbours	10
Work	12
Getting around	16
Shopping and services	18
School and community	20
Entertainment	24
Celebrations	26
Changing times	28
Things to do	30
Index	32

WHERE I LIVE

My name is Eirwen Foulkes. My husband is called John and we have three children: Jack, who is fourteen years old, Elin who's ten and Sara, just four. We live in a village called Penmynydd, which is on the Isle of Anglesey. We call the island *Ynys Môn* in the Welsh language. It is in the county of Gwynedd, in the most northern part of Wales.

Penmynydd is a very scattered village. Fewer than 450 people live in the parish.

There are no big factories, housing estates or busy streets here in Penmynydd, just green fields and small farms. The village has one little shop, which also serves as a post office and filling station.

To the north there is the busy market town of Llangefni. To the south-east is the town of Porthaethwy, called Menai Bridge in English.

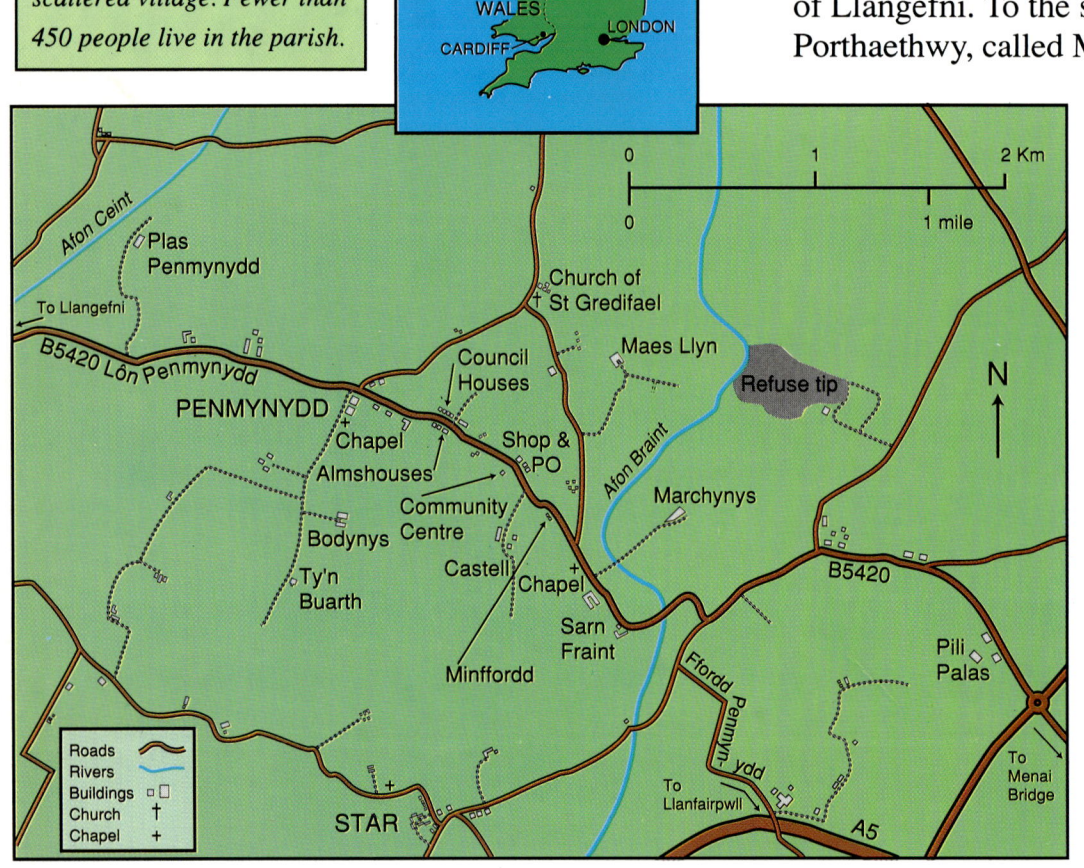

This is the Menai Suspension Bridge, one of the two bridges we can cross to reach the mainland.

To the south of Penmynydd is – wait for it – Llanfairpwllgwyngyllgogerychwyrndrobwll-llantysiliogogogoch! Tourists come to this large village because it has the longest place name in the British Isles. We just call it Llanfairpwll.

LANGUAGE

Welsh is one of the oldest languages in the British Isles. Over half a million people in Wales speak it as their first language and it is the everyday language of most people in Gwynedd. Boxes like this one show you how to pronounce some of the Welsh words in this book.

Cymru CUMM-ree
Eirwen AIR-rr-wen
Gwynedd GWIN-eth (-th as in *the*)
Llanfairpwll Llan-vire-pooll (-ll is a difficult sound for an English speaker. Try putting the tip of your tongue behind your teeth and then breathing out!)
Llangefni Llan-GEV-ni
Marchynys Marrch-UNN-iss (-ch as in Scottish *loch*)
Menai MEN-eye
Penmynydd Pen-MUNN-ith (-th as in *the*)
Porthaethwy Porth-EYE-thwi (-th as in *thing*)

I was born in Penmynydd and grew up on a farm near where I live today. My mother and grandmother still live in the village. John comes from an Anglesey farming family too, although he was born on a farm near Bala, in the mountains of Snowdonia. John's two brothers also have farms on the island. We work our farm and theirs as a single business, so between us we have a fair amount of land.

Our day starts early, with the farming news on Radio Cymru, the BBC's Welsh-language station. There are many farmers on the island and most, like us, speak Welsh as a first language. Nearly two-thirds of all the people on Anglesey are Welsh-speakers and the proportion is higher still in Penmynydd.

Our home is a small farm called Marchynys. John and I have lived here for fourteen years.

Marchynys is a farm of about 70 acres (28 hectares). Most of the farms around here are about the same size. There are wonderful views south to the mountains of Snowdonia, on the mainland.

Anglesey has a mild climate because it has the waters of the Irish Sea all around it. Lambing can start much earlier here than in Snowdonia, where there may still be snow as late as May. Some mountain farmers even send their flocks down to the island for winter grazing.

Anglesey farmers do grow wheat, soft fruit and vegetables, but the Penmynydd soil is quite heavy. On our farm we keep a few cattle – and hundreds of sheep. They say that counting sheep sends you to sleep. It keeps us on our toes! Some farms on Anglesey specialise in pigs, and the farm opposite Marchynys produces only poultry and eggs.

Our neighbour Richard Owen helps John unload a flock of ewes. At busy times such as lambing or shearing we need all the help we can get on the farm.

Meet some of the farm's hardest workers! We have two Welsh collies, Sweep and Siân. It takes at least a year to train a good sheepdog.

LANGUAGE

Gaerwen GUY-rr-wen
Siân Shahn

This sign on the Menai Suspension Bridge means "Anglesey, Mother of Wales". The island was called that because its rich farmland always supplied food to the rest of Wales.

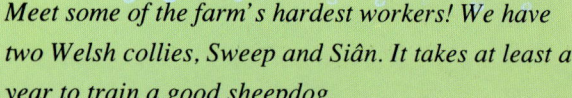

FACTS & FIGURES

The island of Anglesey is about 715 sq km in area. That's about 275 square miles – less than half the size of Greater London.

Each New Year starts with lambing, which normally carries on until April. We need to make the best possible use of the lambing sheds. In the summer we make silage, for feeding the animals through the winter. Large bales are wrapped in black plastic and stored in the farmyard.

The sheep are shorn in June. We hire contract shearers to help us out. All the family lend a hand sorting and packing the wool. After shearing, the sheep are put through a chemical bath. Dipping protects them against blowfly and diseases such as sheep scab. In the autumn the ewes are mated with the rams so there will be lambs for the *next* New Year.

Farming is hard work, but we all enjoy it. It takes up about three-quarters of my time, and John never rests. Jack is old enough to lend a hand, too. He would like to be a farmer when he grows up.

We are members of the F.U.W. (Farmers' Union of Wales). They insure us against any accidents or disasters that might happen on the farm.

December is a busy time, as we sell turkeys for Christmas. This year young children from the village paid the turkeys a visit.

Sara and Elin like the newborn lambs. This season we began lambing in December, about a fortnight earlier than usual.

LLANGEFNI MARKET
EVERY WEDNESDAY

10.30 a.m.	Store and Breeding Pigs.
11.00 a.m.	Barren Cows and Prime Stock (By Weight)
11.00 a.m.	**Stirks and Suckling Calves followed immediately by STORE CATTLE.**
11.30 a.m.	Store Lambs, Breeding Ewes, Rams
11.30 a.m.	Dairy and Breeding Cows
12.00 noon	Rearing Calves and Weanlings

GAERWEN SMITHFIELD
Next collective sale of Farm Implements, Machinery and Tools on Thursday, 27th January at 11 a.m. Entry Forms from the Auctioneers.

GAERWEN SMITHFIELD
STORE STOCK SALE, TUESDAY AT 10.30 a.m.
Please note starting times: 10.30 a.m., Cull Cows, followed by Cows and Calves; 11 a.m., Store Sheep; 12 noon, Store Cattle.

GAERWEN SMITHFIELD
PRIME STOCK SALE, MONDAY AT 11 a.m.
SALE OF 1,000 PRIME LAMBS AND EWES

GAERWEN SMITHFIELD
PRIME STOCK SALE, FRIDAY AT 10 a.m.
SALE OF 300 PRIME CATTLE, 2,000 SHEEP

Livestock is bought and sold at the market town of Llangefni or in the nearby village of Gaerwen.

HOUSING

The oldest house in the village is called Plas Penmynydd. In the Middle Ages it was the home of the Tudors, the family who later went on to rule both England and Wales. The ancestors of Henry VIII and Elizabeth I were born here. Most of the Plas you can see today was built later, between the 1570s and the 1800s.

The *elusendai* (almshouses) are in the care of the Church in Wales. They were built for the elderly people of the parish back in 1620. The ten original dwellings have now been converted into five.

Plas Penmynydd is privately owned and has been restored during the last ten years.

LANGUAGE

Elusendai elli-SEN-dye
Sarn Fraint Sarrn Vrr-eye-nt

The almshouses were built from local materials, with limestone walls and slate roofs.

Most of the farmhouses in Penmynydd were built in Victorian times. Ours is about a hundred years old. Many farms have modern extensions or barns alongside the old stone cattle sheds.

Some local people have built modern bungalows on their land. These are often more comfortable than damp and draughty old farmhouses! Some derelict farm buildings are now being converted into new homes.

At the moment Mary McIntyre and Adrian Brooks live on the mainland, near Bangor. They work locally and have just started converting an old barn into a new home.

There are four council houses at the centre of the village. They were built over sixty years ago to provide villagers with housing at a fair rent.

There has probably always been a farm at Sarn Fraint, by the bridge. Ifor Bowen's family has lived here for about two hundred years. This building was rebuilt in 1810.

The council houses are solidly built. One of them is now privately owned.

Around the coast of Anglesey, retired people from the English cities have bought up a lot of the houses. Other families have bought second homes, which they only live in during the summer. This has pushed up the price of housing so that many young local couples can't afford to buy them. This hasn't really happened in Penmynydd yet. Most people live here all the year round and work locally.

NEIGHBOURS

Here are some of the people I know in the village.

Cyril Hughes lives at Neuadd Lwyd, by the church. He knows as much about what is going on locally as anybody, for he edits a Welsh-language newspaper called *Papur Menai*. Two thousand copies are printed in Llangefni each month. *Papur Menai* is no ordinary newspaper.

Alun Owen lives in the centre of the village, on a farm called Cae Helyg.

"Cae Helyg means 'willow field' in English. I raise calves for the beef-cattle market. I also grow potatoes – and sell them to almost everyone around Penmynydd."

Cyril Hughes

Alun Owen

"We call it a *papur bro* – a community paper. Fifty of these are published in Wales and this one covers the southern part of Anglesey. Its aim is not to make money, but to keep communities together. It features details of village life that are not covered by the larger local papers. One person in each village gathers the news. Word-processing, folding and distribution are all done by local volunteers."

LANGUAGE

Cae Helyg Kye HELL-ig
Minffordd MEAN-forr-th (-th as in *the*)
Neuadd Lwyd NAY-ath LOO-id (-th as in *the*)
Papur bro PAPP-ear brraw

Rose Evans, at Castell, is the local collector of news for *Papur Menai* and President of the Welsh-speaking Penmynydd branch of the Women's Institute. She is also famous with local children – for her cakes.

"I love to make cakes for birthdays and other celebrations. They might be shaped like a train or even a dinosaur! I enjoy decorating some cakes with realistic flowers made of sugar."

The first ever W.I. in Britain was set up just down the road at Llanfairpwll in 1915. We organise all kinds of talks and discussions which are practical as well as interesting."

Dr Gareth Wyn Jones and his wife Ella live just up the road. Their house, Minffordd, is full of books. Gareth's work has taken him all over the world, from Pakistan to North America. Although he lives in rainy Wales, he is an expert on the farming methods used in hot, dry countries. For many years he was based at the University College of North Wales in Bangor.

Dr Gareth Wyn Jones

Gareth now works as chief scientist for the Countryside Council for Wales. "We aim to protect the environment in districts like Penmynydd. We try to find out how the countryside and its wildlife will be affected by new ways of farming or by increased tourism."

Rose Evans

WORK

In some parts of Anglesey there is high unemployment, but most people in Penmynydd have work, in local towns if not in the village itself. One hundred years ago most men on the island worked on farms or went to sea. Today more people work in services, such as tourism or council work. Women worked on the farms too, or as servants in the larger houses.

About one in five people on Anglesey works in industry. Some industries are related to farming. This dairy in Llangefni uses milk to make cheese.

Every farm in Penmynydd used to have its own labourer and often a maid to help with milking or butter-making. Today machinery can do a lot of the heavy farm work.

Many people make a living from farming apart from farmers. For example, there are those who sell feed, fertilisers, fencing, excavators or tractors.

If an animal is ill, we may have to take it to the vet. Alan and Jennifer Finch have a surgery on the road into Llangefni. About half of their work is with pets or riding horses, the rest with farm animals. There used to be more farm work, but over the last twenty years they have seen many small dairy farms close down. The Finches still spend about half their time out on call around Anglesey farms. Lambing is one of the busiest times of the year for them.

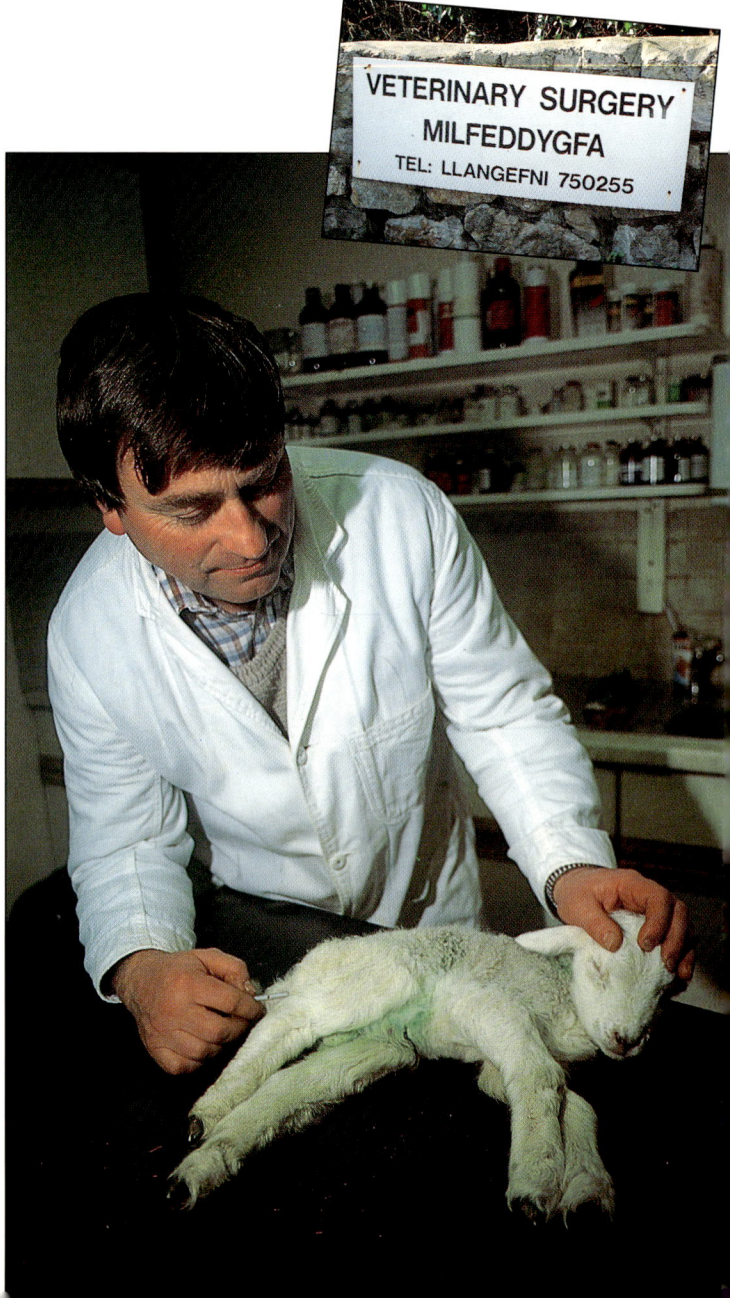

One farm to the east of the village has turned to another kind of farming. It has been made into a "butterfly palace" by its owner, Huw John Hughes. It is called Pili Palas, which is a play on words – it means "butterflies" in Welsh. The old stone barns house a beautiful little garden, heated so that tropical butterflies can flutter around freely. There are birds, snakes and creepy-crawlies, too.

Up to 70,000 tourists now visit the centre between March and December each year. School groups come here to study, and many schools order butterfly eggs for their own breeding programmes.

Pili Palas has its own shop and a café called The Hungry Caterpillar. The centre has five full-time and twelve part-time staff. They are all recruited locally. Tourism does bring money to Anglesey, even if most of the jobs are only seasonal.

To the east of the village there is a large council refuse tip. Council workers dump household rubbish here, filling in the land. Dustcarts come and go all day – so do flocks of scavenging seagulls. Bottles and paper can be brought here for recycling.

An unusual resident in a Welsh farming village – a royal python, cared for by Pili Palas manager Paul Bannister.

Not everyone works in farming. Alun Owen's brother Emyr is a coal merchant. His yard is right in the middle of the village. It is tough work, carrying heavy sacks of coal in all weathers. There are fewer customers than there used to be, and competition is fierce. The business is a joint effort between Emyr and his wife Phyllis, who carries out the administration and all the paperwork.

E. W. OWEN & SON
(E.H. a P.M. OWEN)

Masnachwyr Glo

TY'N PISTYLL
PENMYNYDD   714084

Emyr Owen advertises in the local papers.

Emyr's lorry delivers coal all over the southern part of the island.

Postal deliveries provide a useful link between members of our scattered community. Our postman has a friendly word for everybody.

Some people come to the village for their work. Our postman drives out to Penmynydd each morning from the main sorting office in Bangor. He reaches Marchynys at about 11 a.m.

Just a five-minute drive takes W.P.C. Rhian Davies from Menai Bridge police station to the centre of Penmynydd. She says, "A farming district like this doesn't really give the police any trouble, but we do try to keep in touch with village life. We have one officer who deals with any special problems farmers might have, such as the theft of sheep or cattle. But a lot of our work is routine, like checking licences for moving pigs or keeping a shotgun."

Who else do we see working around Penmynydd? An illness in the family may bring a doctorptomatic on call. Our nearest health centre is at Llanfairpwll. There are six doctors covering a very large area, and they do a wonderful job.

Dr Laura McEwan runs a weekly baby clinic at the health centre in Llanfairpwll.

LANGUAGE

Emyr EM-earr
Rhian HREE-an

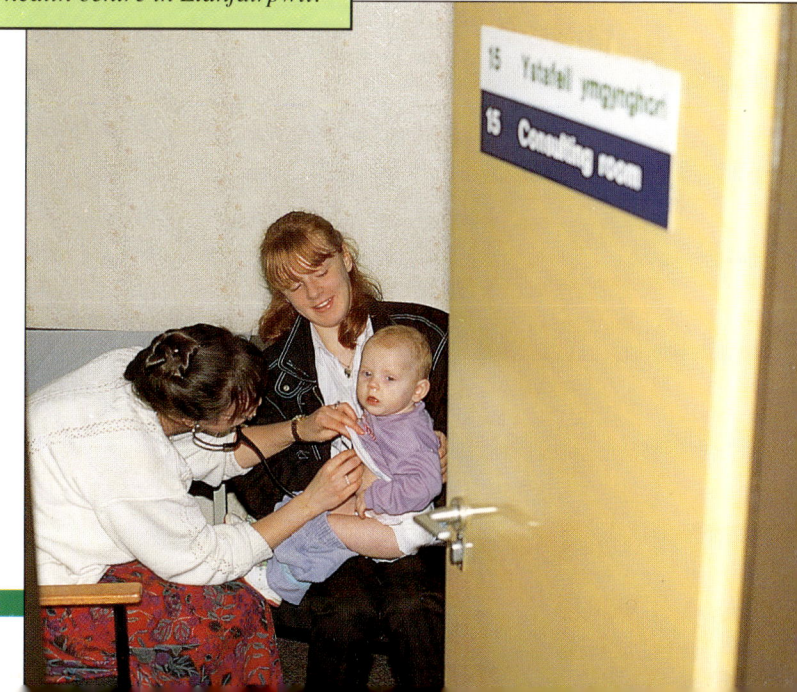

GETTING AROUND

On the farm we get around by Land Rover, motorbike, four-wheeler bike or tractor. We also have a J.C.B. for digging ditches and drains, and a cattle lorry for taking our sheep to market.

Otherwise we drive a car. The back lanes are narrow and often very muddy, with high-banked hedges or stone walls. They are not used much, so grass grows along the middle of them. The hedgerows are full of wildflowers in summer.

The main road, Lôn Penmynydd, is the B5420. It can be very busy with cars. There are no pavements and it's dangerous for children. It is hard to believe that fifty years ago it was so quiet that children could play cricket in the middle of this road. The busiest road is the A5, which borders the west of the village. It carries heavy lorries to Holyhead – the main ferry port for Ireland.

A couple of years ago we blocked the B5420 as a protest against the way drivers speed through our village. As a result, a 40 m.p.h. speed limit was brought in by the council, but some drivers still ignore it.

LANGUAGE

Lôn Lawn

We have to ferry the children around a lot by car. Luckily I can get petrol at the village store.

Big tanker lorries are used to collect the milk from local dairy farms. The words on the front mean "fresh milk".

If you miss the bus, you'll have to wait a week for another one! Apart from school services, there's only one bus a week. It runs through Penmynydd on Thursdays, so that people can visit the street market in Llangefni.

A small steam railway line once passed to the north of the village, through Ceint. That closed years ago. Local diesels still stop at Llanfairpwll, but for Intercity trains we have to go into Bangor, on the mainland. John sometimes travels by train to London, for the Smithfield livestock show. The journey takes about four hours.

SHOPPING AND SERVICES

Support your local village store! That's the message John and I would like to put across. Shops really are at the centre of any small community. We do over half our shopping at Penmynydd's village store and post office.

This is run by Brian and Pat Haddlington, who moved here from Birmingham about five years ago. They are not Welsh speakers, but they have fitted in well and the shop is a meeting place for everyone. Elderly people come here to pick up their pensions, and drivers call by for petrol or newspapers and a chat.

> *The Haddlingtons believe that small shops and sub-post offices should be encouraged by councils and governments. Small businesses keep villages alive.*

Shops in Menai Bridge and Llangefni include bakers, butchers, booksellers, newsagents, ironmongers and grocers. There are banks, restaurants and pubs, and public services such as libraries too – although Elin is really the only keen reader in our family.

Just to the west of Penmynydd is a little village still called Star – despite the fact that the pub from which it takes its name has long since disappeared. Here there is a trading estate, with warehouses selling carpets, doors and double-glazing to passing traffic on the A5.

Once a month we do a big shop at one of the supermarkets in Menai Bridge, Bangor or Llangefni. Sometimes we go on a shopping expedition to Chester. It is only about an hour and a half to the English border, along the A55 coastal expressway.

The post office and store has always been an important meeting place, although its site in the village has changed. Alf Williams was postmaster from about 1954 to 1964.

SCHOOL AND COMMUNITY

The old school in Penmynydd is now used as a community centre but some learning still takes place there. There is an informal nursery school, held twice a week.

Sara goes to this "children's club". Classes are all in the Welsh language. A few of her friends at the club have parents who are English or Irish, but the children soon pick up Welsh without any difficulty.

About a dozen children come to the nursery school each week.

Penmynydd School was built in 1877 but was closed down about forty years ago.

Elin goes to primary school in Llanfairpwll. She likes playing netball. Like many Welsh school children, she is a member of the Urdd. This youth movement organises summer camps, sports, school trips and a junior *eisteddfod*. That is a festival with competitions in poetry, music, singing, dancing (including disco) and painting.

Sara likes playing, making things and hearing stories at the nursery school. Her teacher is called Glenys Roberts.

Last Christmas Elin and her friends were in the primary school play.

LANGUAGE

Eisteddfod eye-STETH-vod
(-th as in *the*)
Urdd Ee-rr-th (-th as in *the*)

Of course, textbooks as well as teaching are in Welsh.

Jack is in the fourth year at the David Hughes comprehensive school in Menai Bridge. His dad is a member of the Parent Teacher Association.

The school bus picks Jack up each day and takes him to school in Menai Bridge.

YSGOL DAVID HUGHES

Jack's favourite subjects are science, technology and maths. All his teaching (except for English) is in Welsh. Children can choose English-language teaching, but they all learn some Welsh. Jack sits his G.C.S.E. next year, and he'd like to go on to study agriculture at the college in Llangefni.

The rector, the Reverend Trefor Evans, lives in Llanfairpwll and comes into Penmynydd to take services.

The first Christian settlement in Penmynydd was a simple hut and well, built by a Celtic saint called Gredifael. That was about 1,500 years ago. The small stone church that stands today was mostly built in the 1300s. The Church in Wales holds a service here each Sunday. It is in Welsh only. Since 1971 our church has been linked with the much busier parish of Llanfairpwll.

The church is a good place to find out about local history. This is the tomb of a medieval knight called Gronw and his wife Myfanwy. They were ancestors of the Tudors. The rose in the window is a badge of the Tudor family.

Chapel preachers came to Penmynydd as early as 1742. At first there were fierce arguments and fights between church-goers and chapel-goers. Most villagers ended up going to chapel. Now we all get on well with each other and sometimes organise joint events.

All the older people in Penmynydd agree about one thing. Fewer people go to church and chapel than in the old days. Congregations may number a dozen or even fewer and the future of the parish church is far from certain.

Penmynydd's Calvinistic Methodist chapel is one of two chapels in the village.

The community is still quite close, though. We meet each other through the schools and through groups like the Women's Institute, or a similar women's organisation called Merched y Wawr.

John was elected to the community council. That is the same as a parish council in England. It deals with all kinds of things that are important to the future of Penmynydd, such as planning and housing.

LANGUAGE

Gredifael GRRED-i-vile
Gronw GRRON-oo
Merched y Wawr MARE-ched er wow-rr (-ch as in Scottish *loch*)
Myfanwy Muv-ANN-wi

ENTERTAINMENT

We lead an outdoor life and don't spend a lot of time in front of the television. Jack exercises Brown, our gun-dog.

A lot of our entertainment is based upon farming. The big event in August is the Anglesey Agricultural Show. John and some other farmers organise the sheep-shearing contest. John was champion himself twenty years ago!

Jack's hobby is .22 target shooting, and his dad John likes shooting game. Jack is a keen member of Penmynydd Young Farmers. Every now and then they organise a stock-judging competition, a play, an eisteddfod, a lamb-roast or a ten-pin bowling trip. It's all great fun.

At the Anglesey Show there are stands and exhibitions of farm machinery, sheepdog trials, shire horses and competitions in ploughing and stock-judging.

Last St Valentine's Day the Young Farmers staged their own Blind Date session in the community centre.

The children may go to see a film at the Plaza Cinema in Bangor. Sometimes John and I go out to dinner. There is a restaurant we like called Castaways that is not too far from here.

LANGUAGE

Fach vah-ch (-ch as in Scottish *loch*)
Pobol y Cwm POB-ol er COOM (-oo as in *wood*)
Sobin a'r Smaeliaid SOBB-in a-rr SMYE-lee-eyed

There is a tiny theatre built in an old barn on the way into Llangefni. It is called Theatr Fach. We go to the pantomime they put on there each Christmas. There is a full-sized theatre in Bangor: Theatr Gwynedd. We saw a play there last month. It was a comedy, based on a popular Welsh TV programme about a football team. We can get four television channels: BBC 1, BBC 2, HTV Wales and S4C. S4C shows mostly Welsh-language programmes.

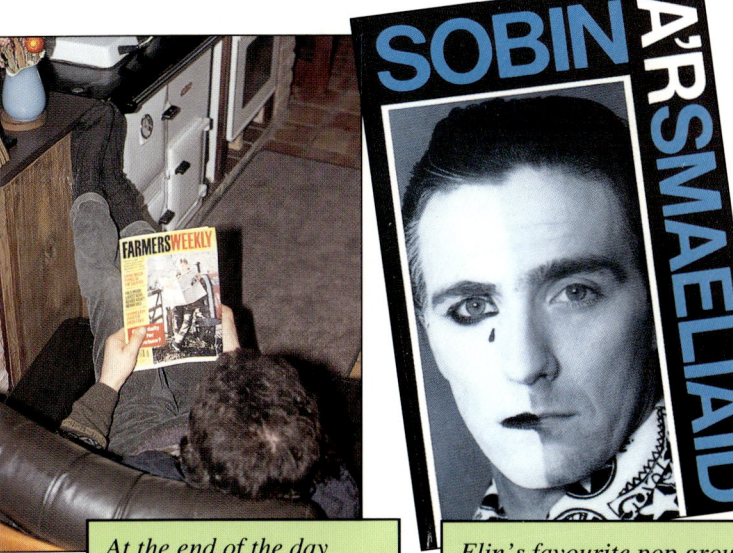

At the end of the day there's a chance to put our feet up and relax.

Elin's favourite pop group is a Welsh band called Sobin a'r Smaeliaid.

Local shops offer a good selection of newspapers and magazines in both Welsh and English.

Our favourite soap opera is called Pobol y Cwm (People of the Valley). It has been running longer than anyone cares to remember.

CELEBRATIONS

Once upon a time the whole village used to gather in the old school to "sing in" the New Year. There's nothing quite like that these days. Local towns have carnivals during the summer and Ffair y Borth – the fair in Menai Bridge – is a must each October.

The fair dates back to 1691. It used to be a place for buying cattle and horses and there were sideshows and wrestling contests. These days it is really just a funfair, but a very big one. On the main fair day it takes over the whole town. There are fortune-tellers and balloon-sellers and stalls selling everything from toffee and china to hammers and nails! The children love it.

Sara still has a birthday party for her friends each year. Jack and Elin prefer a trip to the dry ski slope in Llandudno for their birthday treats.

Sara had four candles on her birthday cake this year. Her birthday party was as noisy as ever!

My uncle, Sam Hughes, hasn't missed Ffair y Borth in 75 years!

LANGUAGE

Ffair y Borth Fire-er-borrth
Llandudno Llan-DID-naw

Ten years ago the National Eisteddfod was held on Anglesey, just a couple of miles from Penmynydd. This festival comes to a different site in the north of Wales every other year, at the beginning of August. All week long there are competitions in poetry and music, plays, pop concerts, exhibitions of art and science, stalls selling Welsh books and music recordings and so on.

There are many old ceremonies at the National Eisteddfod. The leader is called the Archdruid. The red dragon on a green and white background is the flag of Wales.

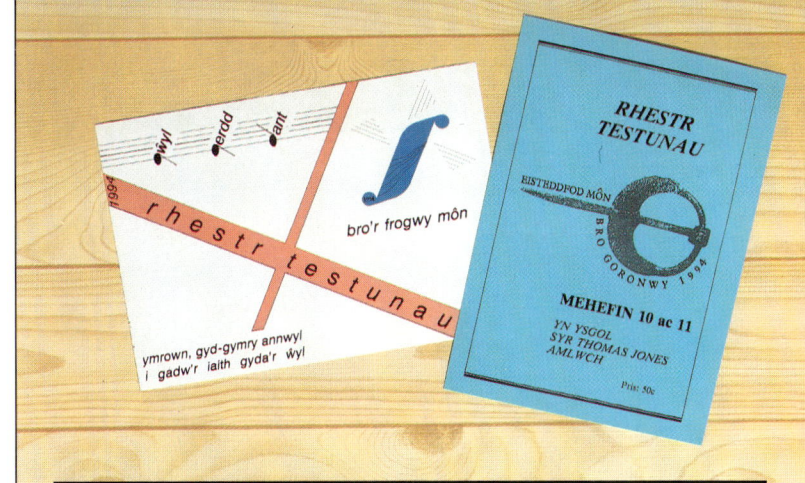

The National Eisteddfod is just the final stage in a series of festivals held locally in villages and regions of Wales throughout the year. These are some of the local programmes.

We don't perform at the Eisteddfod ourselves. We just go along for the day, to meet up with our friends and see what's going on.

Our summer holidays? More farming! We take our caravan down to the Royal Welsh Agricultural Show, in mid-Wales.

CHANGING TIMES

Older people remember when Penmynydd was a very different place. There was chapel and church every Sunday, and on Wednesday nights people went to the Seiat, or Christian fellowship meeting.

Travel into Llangefni – to sell butter or eggs at market – was by pony and trap, or bicycle. Buttermilk was a popular drink in those days, and a ham would hang in the pantry – every family in the village kept a pig. Water came from the farmyard or from the parish pump by the almshouses. There was no electricity.

On Anglesey, sheep used to be washed in the river before shearing.

Horses were used for transport and haulage on the farm.

Haymaking and harvesting were hard work in the old days. But everyone lent a hand.

On the farm, cows were still milked by hand and they were all known by names like "Cochan" (red 'un). Today the cows just have numbers. In the fields there used to be haystacks and old-fashioned threshing machines. And then there were the first tractors. Collecting old tractors is the hobby of Emyr Owen, the coal merchant. He's got eight of them, dating from the 1940s and 50s.

In 1854 a famous writer called George Borrow visited Penmynydd. In his book, *Wild Wales,* he called it "a small village consisting of a few white houses and a mill". Well, the mill has gone, but Penmynydd is still small. What has changed?

Transport has opened up our village. Today people think nothing of travelling to London or going for holidays abroad. Television has put country areas like ours in touch with the cities – there is less difference between us all these days.

FACTS & FIGURES

At the 1991 census, the population of the village was broken down in this way.

0-15 years   16.8%
16-17 years   3.3%
18-pension age 62.0%
pensioners   17.9%

Life is more comfortable than it used to be, I suppose, but is it any better? Perhaps not. But we still have our farming, our language and our sense of community. There are probably as many youngsters in Penmynydd as ever, and that really does give us hope for the future.

LANGUAGE

Cochan COCH-ahn (-ch as in Scottish *loch*)
Seiat SAY-at

Jack's favourite TV programme is Tomorrow's World *on BBC 1, and he has his own computer. In the future computer skills and electronic technology may be as useful to the farmer as sheep-shearing.*

The next generation in Penmynydd! They are likely to see just as many changes as we have.

THINGS TO DO

A WALL DISPLAY
You could make a large display showing the place where you live – like the collage below, which is on display in the old primary school. On it you can see the church, Plas Penmynydd, a Tudor rose, the Menai Suspension Bridge, the refuse tip, the community centre, a woolly sheep and a butterfly from Pili Palas. The words are Welsh for "the Penmynydd environment". What would you include from your neighbourhood on a display?

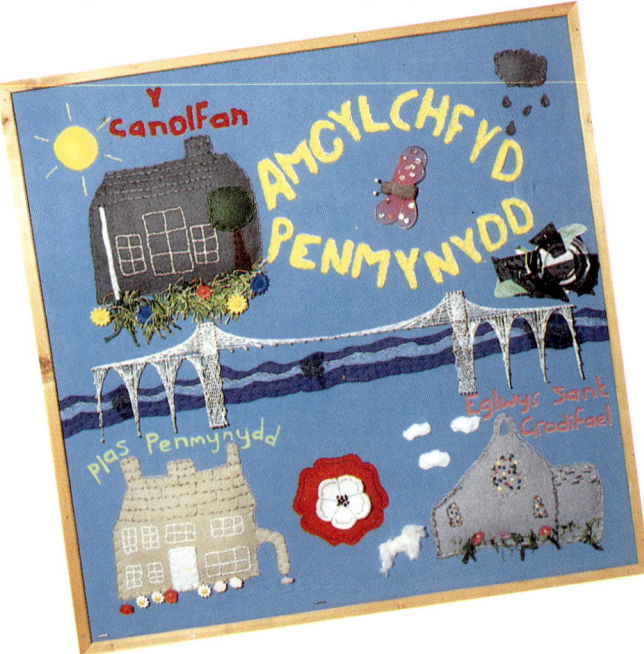

FARMING PRODUCE CHART
The food produced by farms used to be sold locally, at market. Today it may end up far away, on the shelf of a supermarket. Collect all the food labels from your family's weekly shopping. What proportion of goods were produced locally, in your own county or city? What proportion came from other parts of the British Isles? What proportion came from other European countries, and what from other parts of the world? Make a chart showing the results of your survey.

LANGUAGE SURVEY

In Penmynydd everyone speaks Welsh and/or English. But in the nearby city of Bangor you might hear other languages such as French, German, Chinese, Arabic or Bengali. All sorts of languages are spoken in the British Isles. Find out how many different ones are spoken in your neighbourhood.

CHURCHYARD DETECTIVES

In the churchyard at Penmynydd there are beautifully carved slate gravestones. Gravestones and other memorials can tell us how people used to live. Visit your local churchyard, keeping quiet and respecting the feelings of other people there.

Read the words on the stones. When and where did people live? What work did they do? How long did they live? How many children did they have? Can you notice any differences between, say, 150 years ago and the last 20 years?

Is there a war memorial where you live? How many young men died as soldiers, and in which wars?

INDEX

Anglesey Agricultural Show 24

Bangor 19, 25
bus services 17, 21
butterfly farm 13

carnivals 26
celebrations 26-7
chapels 23
cheese making 12
church 22, 23
climate 6
coal merchant 14
community centre 20
community council 23
community life 10, 18, 23
comprehensive school 21
conservation 11
council refuse tip 13
Countryside Council for
  Wales 11

doctors 15

employment 12-15
entertainment 24-5
environment 11

farming
  dairy farms 12, 17
  employment 12
  farm produce 6, 30
  farm size 5
  farm vehicles 16, 28
  Farmers' Union of Wales 7
  lambing 6, 7, 12
  livestock 6, 7
  new technology 29
  sheep shearing 7, 24
  sheepdogs 6
  social events 24
  turkeys 7

Ffair y Borth (fair) 26
filling station 4, 17

health centre 15
hedgerows 16
housing
  almshouses 8
  barn conversions 9
  council houses 9
  farmhouses 8, 9
  new homes 9
  Plas Penmynydd 8
  retirement homes 9

junior eisteddfod 20

Llanfairpwll 5, 15, 17, 22
Llangefni 7, 17, 18, 21, 28
local history 8, 22, 28

map of Penmynydd 4
market 7, 17
Menai Bridge 18, 19, 21, 26
Menai Suspension Bridge 4, 6
milk tankers 17

National Eisteddfod 27
newspaper 10, 11
nursery school 20

police 15
population 4, 29
post office 4, 18, 19
postal services 14
primary school 20

rail services 17
recycling 13
road systems 16
Royal Welsh Agricultural
  Show 27

school bus 21
schools 20-1
shooting 24
shopping 4, 18-19
speed limits 16
Star 19

television 25, 28
theatres 25
things to do 30-1
tourism 11, 12, 13
tractors 28
trading estate 19
transport 16-17, 28

Urdd (youth movement) 20

vet 12
village store 4, 17, 18, 19

Welsh language 5, 10, 20, 21
Women's Institute 11, 23

Young Farmers 24